celebrating st david's day

Elin Meek
translation by Siân Lewis

  GWASG CARREG GWALCH

First published December 2006
© text: Gwasg Carreg Gwalch 2006
© poems: the poets 2006

ISBN 10: 1-84527-016-8
ISBN 13: 978-184527-106-0

Published by Gwasg Carreg Gwalch, 12 Iard yr Orsaf, Dyffryn Conwy, Wales LL26 0EH.
phone 01492642031
fax 01492641502
e-mail llyfrau@carreg-gwalch.co.uk
website: www.carreg-gwalch.co.uk

Original Welsh text
Elin Meek

English text
Siân Lewis

Editor
Gordon Jones

Thanks
To the teachers and pupils of Ysgol Pentreuchaf, Llŷn; Ysgol Bro Plenydd, Four Crosses; Ysgol Rhostryfan; Ysgol Gymraeg Dewi Sant, Llanelli; Ysgol Gymraeg Dewi Sant, Rhyl; Ysgol y Gorlan, Tremadog; Ysgol Dolbadarn, Llanberis; Ysgol Llanbedrog.

To Gaenor Jones, Gwenda Morris a Ruth Jên Evans for the craft ideas. The Perkins family, Rhosgadw, St Davids (daffodil farm). Welsh Tartan Centres, Cardiff. Deiniol Thomas, Menter Iaith Conwy. Gwenfudd James, Caio. Paul Boland, The National Trust, Llanerchaeron. The Very Reverend J. Wyn Evans, Dean, and The Very Reverend Carl Cooper, Bishop of St Davids. Croeso Cymru. Glamorgan Cricket Club. Parc Cenedlaethol Eryri. Brains Brewers, Cardiff. Llanelli Scarlets rugby club. Felinfoel, Llanelli. Riwannon Kervella, Brittany. Rhisiart Hincks. Idris and Lynda Hughes, Comox Valley, Vancouver Island, Canada. Henry Jones-Davies, Cambria. Dewi Pws. Twm Morys. Iwan Llwyd. Meirion McIntyre Huws. Anne Hunt, Manchester Welsh Society. Gareth G. Jones formerly of Taiwan. David Price, Arizona. Katharine Lewis, Alberta, Canada. Angela Evans, Atlanta, Georgia. Dilys Anderson, Melbourne, Australia. Catrin Brace, New York. Lynda Ganatsiou, Greece.

Photographs
© Myrddin ap Dafydd: 21, 46, 48, 49ch, 54, 60, 61t&c, 64t & bl, 65cl, cr, bl; 70, 71, 74, 75bl.
© Croeso Cymru: 49t, 66.
© Sion Ilar: 64br
© Elin Meek: 8–10, 17, 42, 47l, 51l, 56l, 72l.
© Glamorgan Cricket Club: 52
© Arvid Parry Jones: 50, 51l, 58–9, 67t.
© Deiniol Thomas: 74.
© Keith Morris: 75.
© Photolibrary Wales: 40–1, 47l.
© Cambria: 65bl, 75t, 78b.
© Ysgol Gymraeg Dewi Sant, Llanelli 44, 72bl.
© National Library of Wales: 61bl & r, 63b.

Illustrations
© James Field: 6–9, 11–16, 18.
© Graham Howells: 4, 5, 10, 19–20, 22–31, 33, 34.
© Robin Lawrie: 36–9, 43, 45–6, 52, 54–5, 68–9.
© Gelder Design & Mapping: 37

Crafts
© Ruth Jên Evans: 50–1, 58–9.

Design
Welsh Books Council

The publishers wish to acknowledge the support of the Welsh Books Council

Printed in Belgium by Proost

contents

introduction

St David, patron saint of Wales. This is the great man, known in Welsh as Dewi Sant, whom we remember every year on the 1st of March. Welsh people celebrate his life in various ways, not only in Wales, but throughout the world. In this book we shall look at those celebrations and try to answer a number of questions. For example, who exactly was St David? Why do we remember him in this way? Why do we wear a daffodil or a leek and wave the red dragon flag? How did the Welsh costume develop? We'll also suggest a few things you can do on St David's Day.

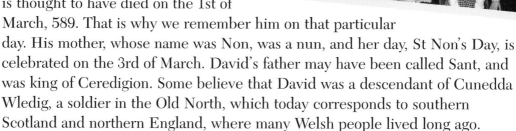

Nearly fifteen hundred years have gone by since the time of St David. Very few firm facts are known about him. He lived in the sixth century, and is thought to have died on the 1st of March, 589. That is why we remember him on that particular day. His mother, whose name was Non, was a nun, and her day, St Non's Day, is celebrated on the 3rd of March. David's father may have been called Sant, and was king of Ceredigion. Some believe that David was a descendant of Cunedda Wledig, a soldier in the Old North, which today corresponds to southern Scotland and northern England, where many Welsh people lived long ago.

4

David lived in south Ceredigion and north Pembrokeshire, and especially in the area known today as St Davids. He was a monk, and founded a monastery at Mynyw (or Menevia), the old name for St Davids. It seems he was buried in the grounds of that monastery, where St Davids Cathedral stands today.

Everything else we know about David is either legend or folk tale. The people of his time realised he was an exceptional man, so after his death they made up strange and wonderful stories about him. It didn't matter whether these stories were true or not. Their one aim was to show how extraordinary he was. These stories all describe David as an exemplary man who believed in God, cared for others and led his people.

The oldest known book which mentions David is *Buchedd Dewi* (The Life of David). It was written in 1090 by Rhygyfarch, Bishop of St Davids, five hundred years after the death of David. So it probably contains a mixture of historical fact and stories that had sprung up over the centuries.

the age of the saints

The Age of the Saints was a very interesting period in Welsh history. In the sixth century Christianity had only just reached Wales. It was a new and exciting religion. To begin with, people from the Mediterranean brought Christianity to the Celtic lands of Brittany, Ireland, Wales, Cornwall, Scotland and the Isle of Man. Then young men and women from the most important families in these lands travelled from country to country to spread the news about Jesus Christ and God. They would walk from place to place along ancient paths and crossed the sea in small ships. It was a time of great activity and enthusiasm, which lasted for five hundred years.

These people were called saints, because they lived as monks and nuns, and were considered holy, or saintly. The Celtic saint would leave his or her town or village and withdraw to a quiet place to live a simple life. There the saint would set up a 'cell' or a 'llan', which consisted of a shelter in which to live and a plot of land on which to grow food. He or she would pray, read the Bible and make copies of it, and also fast (living on water alone, without food). The saints would preach in their locality, and gradually other people would come and join them. Then more cells had to be built, and more land cleared to grow food. Very often they would also erect a building to shelter travellers and the sick.

the saints settle down

So, gradually, a small community would form, and they would build a chapel of wood or stone where all the members of the community could come together to pray regularly. Some communities were small, with around ten members. Others were huge, with a membership of hundreds or even thousands of monks and nuns. A community was often known by the name of its founding saint, which in Wales was preceded by the word 'Llan': for example Llandeilo (Teilo); Llanarmon (Garmon); Llanilltud (Illtud).

Gallarus Oratory Celtic Church, Dingle, Kerry, Ireland

Women played an important role in these Celtic communities, and sometimes there were women in charge. A number of Welsh place names – such as Llanelli (St Elli) and Llanddwyn (St Dwynwen) – are proof of this. Dwynwen founded her community on an island (Llanddwyn Island), and other saints also lived on islands: Cybi (Ynys Cybi, or Holy Island), Seiriol (Ynys Seiriol, or Puffin Island) and Cwyfan for example.

The monks and nuns met once a day to worship, and then returned to their cells to pray and to study. The study of the Psalms was very important to the Celtic saints. They learnt every one of the hundred and fifty psalms by heart, and sometimes they would have to recite fifty of them at a time. It sounds much worse than reciting in the Urdd Eisteddfod . . .

St Cwyfan's Church

the lives of the saints

The great monasteries attracted pupils – the children of royal families and local landowners – who came to learn to read, write, sing and enjoy literature, art and music. The pupils also worked on the land, prayed and studied. The monastery was a form of boarding school for rich children of that time. Crosses were often erected near the *llannau*. There are many excellent examples in Wales. One of the oldest is a stone on Caldey Island near Tenby. On the stone is set a cross, and underneath the cross is a message in the Ogham alphabet and also in Latin asking passers-by to pray for a saint called Cadog. Many of the crosses are very tall, with intricate patterns – such as the cross at Nevern in the north of Pembrokeshire.

Nevern Cross

There are many other treasures associated with the Age of the Saints, such as the 'Book of Kells' which was written and illuminated on the island of Iona in Scotland, then later moved to a monastery in Kells in Ireland.

Wales was famous for saints such as Dyfrig, who was an Abbot on Caldey Island. Illtud too was famous in his day. Many pupils came to Llanilltud Fawr (Llantwit Major) to study philosophy, scripture, poetry, art and arithmetic. One of Illtud's pupils was Samson, who went to live in Dyfrig's community on Caldey Island. Samson then went to Ireland, Cornwall and Brittany, carrying all his books in a cart. But the most famous of all the Welsh saints was, of course, David.

BEFORE DAVID'S BIRTH

Many tales about David relate to the period before his birth, and are meant to show that he was a very special saint. It is said that the wizard Merlin foresaw David's birth. Also, according to legend, Patrick, the patron saint of Ireland, was foretold of David's birth. Patrick wanted to found a community in St Davids, but an angel told him that another saint would do so in thirty years' time. Perhaps the purpose of this tale is to show that for the people of Wales, David is a more important saint than Patrick. The remains of Patrick's chapel can be seen near Whitesands, St Davids.

Around this time an angel appeared to Sant, King of Ceredigion, and told him that a very special son would be born to him in thirty years' time. The angel told Sant that while he was hunting on the banks of the River Teifi, he would receive three gifts. Firstly, as he approached the riverbank, he would kill a stag. Secondly, while fishing, he would catch a large salmon. Thirdly, he would come across a colony of bees with combs that were dripping with sweet honey.

The stag was a sign that Sant's son would be a strong man, who could conquer all evil. Like the salmon, his son would lead a simple life, able to live on bread and water and not grow fat like those who lived on meat and rich food. The honey was a sign that he would be a very wise man. Lastly the angel asked Sant to take a portion of the stag, the salmon and the honeycomb to the monastery of Tŷ Gwyn on the slopes of Carn Llidi near St Davids (or, some say, to Mawgan monastery near the River Teifi).

Sant was delighted with this news. Off he rode towards the River Teifi. Soon he saw a large stag running in the woods. He raised his bow and arrow, took careful aim, and shot the animal dead. This was the first of the gifts, and Sant was overjoyed. The angel had obviously told the truth.

Then Sant knelt on the bank of the Teifi and wondered how he could catch a salmon. He rested his hands on the grass, and felt a spear beneath his fingertips! He picked it up and, almost at once, saw a salmon flashing towards him. He threw the spear and pierced the fish. Now he had two gifts.

Suddenly Sant heard the hum of bees. They had settled in the hollow trunk of a nearby tree. Sant wasn't too fond of bees, but he risked putting his hand into the hole. When he pulled out the comb, it was dripping with honey. Sant was very pleased indeed. He had had his three gifts.

Gratefully he went to the monastery, taking with him the stag, the salmon and the honeycomb, which he gave to the monks as gifts. Everything the angel had told him had come true. Now he would have to wait thirty years till the birth of his son.

Gildas loses his voice

While Non was expecting David, she had nothing to eat and drink but bread and water. She went regularly to church to pray. One morning, when her baby was almost due, she went to listen to Gildas preaching. Gildas was one of the most famous Welsh saints.

When Gildas got up to preach, not a word came from his lips. He couldn't speak. He made everyone leave the church, because he realised something was wrong. Perhaps he'd be able to preach once the church was empty. For a second time he got up to give his sermon. But once again he failed.

"Is there still someone in the church?" asked Gildas.

He saw someone coming towards him from a dark corner of the church. It was Non.

"Non," said Gildas, "you are expecting a son who will be a far greater saint than I. So I cannot preach while you remain in the church."

That was when Non realised she was carrying a very special baby.

In the meantime Non's father, King Cynyr, had been watching her closely. He knew that Non was expecting a baby and he wanted to know what sort of child it would be. He went to a wizard who told him that Non would have a son. That son would be a wise and strong man, even wiser and stronger than the king.

Cynyr was furious when he heard the wizard's words. He didn't want Non to have a baby who was wiser and stronger than he was. He decided to follow Non – and as soon as the baby was born he would kill the child.

the birth of david

By this time Non was in labour, for the baby was about to be born. But a wild storm blew up, which kept King Cynyr at bay. The rain lashed, the wind roared and lightning rent the sky. All of a sudden the sun broke through the clouds and lit up the place where Non was giving birth to her son. Non held on so tightly to a rock that she left on it the imprint of her hand, as though on soft clay.

As the baby was born, lightning fell from the sky, struck the rock where Non was lying and split it in two. One half leapt into the air and landed on the ground at her feet. On the very spot where it landed a church was built, called Capel Non (Non's Chapel). The ruins can still be seen on the coast near St Davids, as well as a spring that appeared when David was born. At one time the water from this spring was used in the cathedral.

Present-day
Non's Church

Non's Well

Ruins of the original
Non's Chapel

David's Christening

David was christened in Porth Clais, near St Davids, where the River Alun flows into the sea. As Bishop Aelfyw (who may have been David's cousin) baptised him, the water splashed into the eyes of Movi, a blind monk who was holding the baby. Movi's sight was restored and a spring appeared on the very spot where they stood. Today it is known as Ffynnon Ddewi (David's Well), although only a small stream remains.

It's strange how often springs or wells feature in these stories. We tend to take water for granted. But in that day and age, when people did not have a supply of water to their homes, wells were very important. If they dried up, people died of thirst. People also believed that some wells were holy and that their waters could cure disease – especially eye diseases and rheumatism.

David's education

In the sixth century, few children had any schooling, but since David came from an important family, he was lucky enough to be educated. It seems that he first went to Henfynyw School, near Aberaeron, or Tŷ Gwyn, on the slopes of Carn Llidi near St Davids. Every day, while he was at school, a dove with a golden beak would land on David's shoulder and play around him.

After a while David moved on to a school run by a monk called Paulinus, who was a famous teacher in his day. The school was at the monastery in Llanddeusant, which is now in north Carmarthenshire. Poor Paulinus was losing his sight and his eyes were very painful. He asked David to lay his hands on his face to cure him, and indeed, when David did so, Paulinus's sight was restored.

david's missionary work

David spent time with Paulinus reading the Bible and learning how to spread the good news about Jesus Christ. A person who spreads 'the good news' or gospel is known as a missionary. There was much missionary work to be done, so David went on a journey through south Wales and the west of England. At that time it was no easy journey, for thick forest covered much of the land, and travelling was extremely difficult. To succeed you had to be very determined – and David was a very determined man. He had a vision. He wanted to set the Celtic Church on firm foundations and spread the news about Jesus Christ.

David is said to have worn rough clothes, tied with a rope. Hanging from a band was a loud bell. This bell was so famous, it had a name: Bangu. *Ban* means 'high' as in Bannau Brycheiniog (the Brecon Beacons), which means 'high mountains'. And *cu* or *gu* means 'dearly loved', as in *mam-gu* ('grandmother', or 'dear mother') and *tad-cu* ('grandfather', or 'dear father'). People were pleased to hear the loud and much-loved sound of Bangu and they would crowd around David to listen to him preach.

david's churches

Around sixty churches have been dedicated to David. Many are called 'Llanddewi'. Every one of them lies south of Llanrhystud and Glasbury. Some are in towns and villages that are now in England – in Gloucestershire and Somerset – and there are eight in Devon and Cornwall. At that time a form of old Welsh was spoken in these areas, before the Angles and the Saxons came and attacked the Welsh.

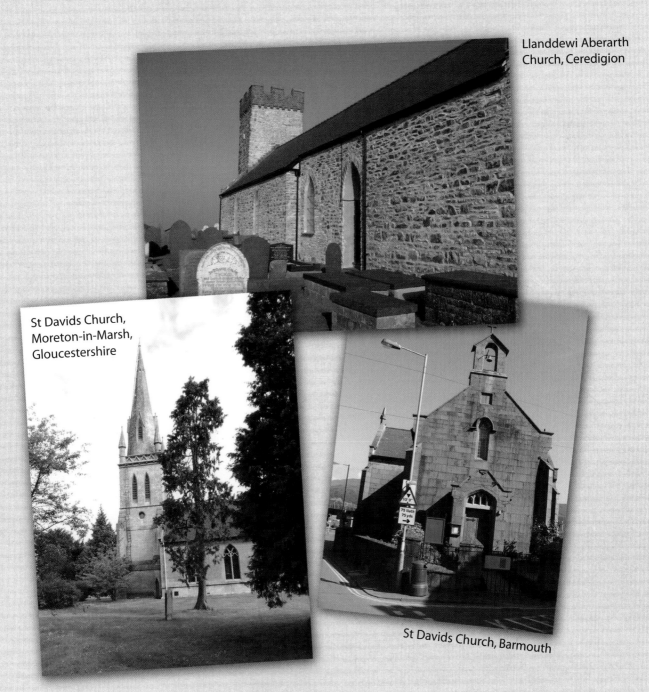

Llanddewi Aberarth Church, Ceredigion

St Davids Church, Moreton-in-Marsh, Gloucestershire

St Davids Church, Barmouth

setting up a community in Glyn Rhosyn

Soon David wanted to set up his own community. Legend tells that an angel led him to the area known as Mynyw, where St Davids stands today. David chose to settle in Glyn Rhosyn (Rose Vale), on the banks of the River Alun.

Unfortunately, someone was already living there: an important Irishman called Boia. Boia was the local chieftain and he lived opposite Glyn Rhosyn in an empty Iron Age hill fort, which is known today as Clegyr Boia. Of course he wasn't at all happy to see the smoke of David's fire swirling over the land. At that time, anyone who lit a fire in a particular area could lay claim to all the land that was covered by the smoke. And this was a big fire! No wonder Boia was furious.

Boia and his wife Satrapa decided to gather their men and drive David from the land. There were many of them, and they should have easily defeated David and his small band of monks. However, when Boia's men spotted David with his monks, they could not fight against him. All they could do was mock him and call him names. As they walked back to the fort, they saw all Boia's animals lying dead in the fields. This scared Boia: it was obvious that David was a remarkable man with magical powers. Boia went back to apologise to David, and indeed, by the time he'd walked back to his fort, David had restored all the animals to life and they were peacefully grazing as usual.

So Boia agreed to give Glyn Rhosyn to David, but Satrapa wasn't at all happy, and decided to plot against him. To tempt the monks, she sent some naked young women to swim in the River Alun. This plan failed. Her next plot was to lure her stepdaughter, Dunod, to Glyn Rhosyn to gather nuts. She told Dunod to bow her head, so she could brush her hair. But when the girl did so, Satrapa drew a knife and cut Dunod's throat as a sacrifice to her gods, and as a curse upon David. But when a spring welled up from the very spot where Dunod's blood had been shed, it was a sign that David's God was more powerful than her own. Boia's wife ran away, and she disappeared as though the earth had swallowed her.

Boia blamed David for the death of his daughter and the disappearance of his wife, so he had to take revenge. He decided to attack David under cover of darkness. But that very night another Irishman called Lisci launched an attack on Boia's own camp, and he cut off Boia's head. A fire from heaven devoured the camp. At last David could live in safety in Glyn Rhosyn. The small beach of Porth Lisci, near St Davids, is still a reminder of Lisci, the Irishman.

david's life in glyn rhosyn

It's very difficult for us today to imagine how people lived in the sixth century. Life was much less busy in many ways, but still there was plenty to do. What do we know about the lives of David and his monks? Well, they had to cultivate the land, and they appear to have done so without the help of oxen, let alone the machines we use today. So it was slow, backbreaking work with pick and shovel. The clothes they wore were made out of coarse material, but their heads and feet were bare, even when they worked. The two meals they ate each day were made up of the vegetables they grew themselves, along with a little bread and salt. It is said they never ate meat. A lot of food was given to the poor people of the area, and to elderly widows who could not grow their own food.

Legend claims that David and his followers did not drink wine, and that water, or a mixture of water and milk, was all that they drank in Glyn Rhosyn. Perhaps that is why David was given the name 'Waterman', though some say it was because he liked to discipline himself by standing up to his armpits in cold water. Another possible explanation for the name was that David had opened several wells – up to thirty in all – which were considered holy.

As well as cultivating the land, the monks would read and pray, and spend time welcoming and giving shelter to pilgrims who came to Glyn Rhosyn. Many of the pilgrims followed ancient paths, which dated from the Bronze Age, and several of the churches dedicated to David are built along these paths. There was a lot of activity around St Davids, and a lot of coming and going at this time. Some pilgrims came across the sea, and it is likely that the sea would have been full of little boats sailing between Wales, Ireland, Cornwall and Brittany.

the plot to kill david

One of the strangest stories about David tells of a plot against his life. The story begins in Ireland on the night before Easter. On that night an angel appeared to St Aidan, one of David's former pupils. The angel's message was grim. Three wicked monks were plotting to poison David on Easter Sunday. Poor Aidan felt totally helpless. How could he warn David before it was too late? Easter Sunday was the very next day, he was separated from Glyn Rhosyn by a stretch of sea, and there was no time for him to sail across. The angel told him not to worry, but to send one of his disciples to the beach instead.

So Aidan sent his disciple, Sguthyn, who walked into the sea till the water reached his knees. At that point a monster rose from the waves and carried Sguthyn on his back to Porth Clais, the little harbour near Glyn Rhosyn. They reached shore by midday on Easter Sunday. Sguthyn ran to Glyn Rhosyn and reached the monastery in time to warn David of the plot just as the monks were sitting down in the refectory to eat their midday meal.

One of the wicked monks came to serve David. He was carrying bread – poisoned bread. Sguthyn was about to warn David again, when David broke the bread into three pieces. He gave the first piece to a dog that was standing outside the door. As soon as the creature ate the bread, it died. It lost all its fur, and its stomach split and spilled its contents all over the floor. It was a terrible sight, and proof that the poison was exceptionally strong. Then David gave the second piece to a crow that was sitting on a nest in an ash tree between the refectory and the River Alun. As soon as it had swallowed the bread, the bird fell from the tree and was dead by the time it hit the ground.

There was one piece of bread left, and every single person in the refectory was watching David. Would he make one of the wicked monks eat the bread? No. David blessed the last piece and ate it himself. The monks held their breath, but to their great relief, nothing happened. David told everyone present of the plot to kill him. The wicked monks were cursed and everyone thanked God for saving David.

the miracles of llanddewi brefi

A dispute arose among church people in Wales, and Paulinus, David's old teacher, wanted him to settle the argument by addressing a meeting in a place that later became known as Llanddewi Brefi. David had twice refused to go there, although two other saints, Deiniol and Dyfrig, begged him to attend.

In the end, Deiniol and Dyfrig went to Glyn Rhosyn to persuade David to return with them to Llanddewi Brefi. David's followers went to a lot of trouble to provide the two men with a good meal. According to legend, as they were carrying water from the well, the water turned into wine before they reached the monastery refectory. Since David and his monks did not drink wine, this was a stroke of luck! But after all the preparations, Deiniol and Dyfrig refused to eat a bite of food until David had promised to go with them to Llanddewi Brefi. When he saw how determined his friends were, David had to agree.

On the way, as they were nearing the River Teifi, David met a woman who was grieving. Her son had just died, and she begged David to go with her to the house where her son's body lay. David did so, and prayed to God to restore the son to life. The son's eyes opened as if he were waking from sleep, and he stood up. He became one of David's followers and stayed with him for many years. A spring, called David's Well, sprang from the spot where the miracle took place.

By the time they reached Llanddewi Brefi, a huge crowd was waiting for them. No one could see David, but even so, David refused to walk to a nearby hill where he would be within sight of everyone. The people were worried: if they couldn't see David, surely they wouldn't be able to hear him. But David began to preach on the flat ground where he stood, and everyone was astonished that his voice was so loud and clear. Then David placed a cloth beneath his feet and all of a sudden, as he was preaching, the ground rose and formed a tall hill. So now everyone could see him and hear him. Then a white dove, a symbol of the Holy Spirit, landed on his shoulder. Everyone was astonished at these miracles, and David's fame grew.

a pilgrimage to Jerusalem

Like many of his contemporaries, David went on a pilgrimage to Jerusalem. Legend tells that David was informed by an angel that he should go, and Teilo and Padarn accompanied him. David was made an archbishop by the Patriarch in Jerusalem, and the three of them were given valuable gifts. Teilo was given a bell, Padarn was given a stick and a tunic threaded with gold, and David was given an altar.

the death of saint david

According to tradition David was told by an angel at the end of February 589 that he would soon die. He would be carried to heaven, and he had to prepare himself. The following Sunday, he preached to his followers for the last time. According to the book *Buchedd Dewi*, these are some of the most important words contained in that sermon:

"Lords, brothers and sisters, be joyful and keep your faith and belief, and do the little things that you have heard me talk about and seen me do."

David died on the 1st of March 589. No one knows exactly how old he was when he died. It's said that the monastery in Glyn Rhosyn was filled with sweet scents and the sound of angel voices as Jesus Christ received the soul of David into heaven that day.

the cult of david grows

After David died, he was not forgotten. On the contrary, he became more popular than ever. Pilgrims would flock to St Davids. The most exciting things on display were David's possessions: St John's Gospel in his handwriting, his stick, the altar given to him in Jerusalem, his clothes, and Bangu, his bell. According to tradition some of these things were also kept in other churches throughout Wales, such as at Llanddewi Brefi, Llangyfelach near Swansea, and Glasgwm in Powys.

David's body was buried in the grounds of the monastery of Glyn Rhosyn, but the bones were dug up some four hundred years after his death when it became fashionable to make a pilgimage to see the bones of saints and touch them in the hope of obtaining a cure from disease.

The poem *Armes Prydain*, which was written around 930, describes David as a saint and leader of the Welsh. One line of the poem talks of raising David's flag: 'And they will raise holy David's banner' (*A lluman glân Dewi a ddyrchafant*).

David was made a Saint by Pope Calixtus II in 1123. The 1st of March became part of the Church calendar. The Pope also announced that two pilgrimages to St Davids was equal to one to Rome, and that three pilgrimages to St Davids was equal to one pilgrimage to Jerusalem. St Davids became a very popular place for pilgimage in the Middle Ages.

famous abroad

Here are two lines, which may have once been an early advertisement to persuade pilgrims to make two journeys to St Davids rather than one to Rome (Mynyw is the old name for St Davids).

'Twice to Mynyw and once to Rome.
You'll profit as much while closer to home.'
(*Dos i Rufain unwaith ac i Fynyw ddwywaith,*
Yr un elw cryno a gei di yma ag yno.)

In the twelfth century, David became popular in two other Celtic countries, namely Brittany and Ireland. Nine churches were dedicated to him in Brittany and many places in Ireland are associated with him, including Davidstown in Kilkenny, and a holy well dedicated to David in Oylgate. In this way David became a very important Celtic saint.

In the sixteenth century, the Protestant Reformation came to England and Wales. Henry VIII decided to establish a state church and break away from the Church of Rome. Anything connected with the Church of Rome was prohibited and no one was allowed to celebrate saints' days. Once again St David's Day was forgotten. But in the eighteenth century people began to celebrate St David's Day once more, and it is still celebrated today.

St Divi (St David) Chapel in Plouneour-Menez, Britanny

The well of St Divi in Dirinonn, Britanny

The statue of St Divi in the well

32

the miracles of st david

There's too much poverty,
The children say.
Make us a miracle,
David, today!
Make all of us brothers
And sisters mild
To the penniless widow
And orphan child.

There's too much fighting,
The children say.
Make us a miracle,
David, today!
Send us a gentle
And golden-beaked dove,
To stop the wars
And bring peace and love.

There's too much sickness,
The children say.
Make us a miracle,
David, today!
Send us the medicine
From your holy spring,
To make us all better,
To make us all sing.

There's too much cruelty,
The children say.
Make us a miracle,
David, today!
Make all the hunting dogs
Turn around
And lead the foxes home
Safe and sound.

There's too much guzzling,
The children say.
Make us a miracle,
David, today!
Please let us all
Be more like you,
Who enjoyed plain bread
And water too.

Adapted from 'Gwyrthiau Dewi'
written by the children of Ysgol Bro
Plenydd, Y Ffôr, and Twm Morys

33

pilgrimages

In St David's time, and in the Middle Ages, going on a pilgrimage was part of everyday life. The people who went on pilgrimages – the pilgrims – travelled great distances to visit holy places. Sometimes they would even cross the sea, as did David, Teilo and Padarn when they went to Jerusalem. Rome, Jerusalem and Santiago de Compostela in northern Spain were the main destinations overseas.

Pilgrims had many different reasons for going on their journeys. At that time, people didn't live very long because there was so much illness and disease, and there were no cures as there are today. So some went in search of a cure, and they would drink water from holy wells and pray at various churches along the way. Those who were too ill to travel would send someone else on a pilgrimage on their behalf. Other pilgrims were hoping for forgiveness of sins, in case they suffered the fires of purgatory and the tortures of hell after their deaths.

To some, the pilgrimages were an excuse for travelling, seeing new places and meeting new people. These may well have been the first 'holidays' and the pilgrims the first 'tourists'. Other people entertained the pilgrims along the way – by singing, juggling or doing tricks – while others begged for money.

There were many dangers on these long journeys, which sometimes involved travelling through a foreign land. The terrain could be difficult, thieves would lie in wait, and pilgrims sometimes fell ill and died far from home.

A pilgrim was easily recognisable by his dress: a grey woollen cloak, loosely tied around the waist, with a hood sewn around the neck. On his head he wore a wide-brimmed black or grey hat. He would carry a stick to help him cross rough ground and protect him from thieves. He would have a little satchel to carry his money, his belongings, and maybe instructions on how to reach his destination.

the journeys of the pilgrims

The pilgrims visited four main centres in Wales: Holywell (which is now in Flintshire) to visit St Winifred's Well; Bardsey Island, where 20,000 saints lie buried; Penrhys (in the Rhondda) to see a well dedicated to the Virgin Mary, and St Davids. The paths linking these places were busy. The path from Holywell to St Davids, for instance, crossed Wales and was 156 miles in length. It was quite a journey, especially for the poor pilgrims who had to walk barefoot (rich pilgrims would ride on horseback). Some sailed to the harbours near St Davids. Others, on their way from St Davids to Bardsey Island, would choose to walk as far as Fishguard, Cardigan or Mwnt, near Cardigan, and then sail across Cardigan Bay.

Along the way there were many places that offered lodgings, shelter and care to the pilgrims. Monasteries and abbeys offered shelter – such as St Dogmael's Abbey near Cardigan, or Strata Florida and Margam – and sometimes a hospice (*ysbyty*) was erected for that purpose, such as Ysbyty Ystwyth in Ceredigion and Ysbyty Ifan in Denbighshire. Pilgrims on their way to Bardsey Island used to meet in St Beuno's Church in Clynnog Fawr. There they would visit Beuno's well, where they left white stones to show they had passed by. They would then have a meal in Y Gegin Fawr inn before crossing the strait to Bardsey.

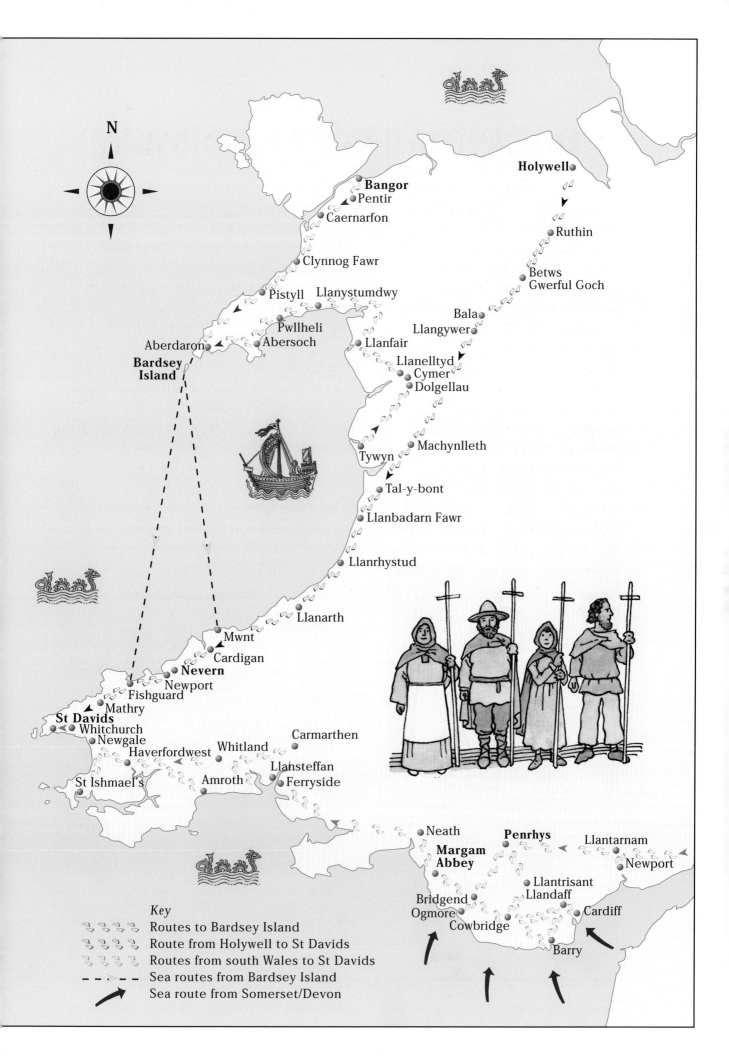

N

Holywell

Bangor
Pentir
Caernarfon

Ruthin

Clynnog Fawr

Betws
Gwerful Goch

Pistyll   Llanystumdwy

Pwllheli
Abersoch

Bala
Llangywer

Aberdaron

Llanfair

Bardsey
Island

Llanelltyd
Cymer
Dolgellau

Machynlleth

Tywyn

Tal-y-bont

Llanbadarn Fawr

Llanrhystud

Llanarth

Mwnt
Cardigan

Nevern
Newport
Fishguard
Mathry

St Davids
Whitchurch
Newgale
Haverfordwest   Whitland   Carmarthen

St Ishmael's   Amroth   Llansteffan
Ferryside

Neath   Penrhys   Llantarnam

Margam
Abbey   Newport

Llantrisant
Llandaff
Bridgend   Cardiff
Ogmore
Cowbridge

Barry

Key
Routes to Bardsey Island
Route from Holywell to St Davids
Routes from south Wales to St Davids
Sea routes from Bardsey Island
Sea route from Somerset/Devon

pilgrims from far away

Some pilgrims came from the south-west of England. They sailed across the sea to Kidwelly and then followed the path to St Davids. As they approached St Davids, the pilgrims from the north would pass through Nevern (in north Pembrokeshire). That is where the pilgrims who were too ill to reach St Davids would wait for their death. One of the pilgrim paths in Nevern leads to a cross carved in the rock above the village. Beneath the cross, there is a stone that has been worn away by pilgrims kneeling to pray. Small crosses can also be seen in holes in the rock.

Some six miles from St Davids there is a little village called Mesur y Dorth (the Measure of the Loaf). This is the name of a stone that is set in a wall by the roadside. According to one tradition, this is where the pilgrims used to eat bread for the last time before reaching St Davids. Perhaps they measured the loaf they had brought with them to see if they had enough food to last them for the rest of the journey.

Another tradition about the stone tells of a great famine. St David, or maybe the Bishop of St Davids, said that no one was to bake a loaf that was larger than the circle on the stone. Close to St Davids stands Maen Dewi, a standing stone, where pilgrims used to gather. There are dozens of wells around St Davids where pilgrims would drink holy water, and the remains of many of them can still be seen. You can also walk along some of the paths, although many have disappeared beneath our modern roads.

Today, in St Davids Cathedral, there is little to show what happened to the pilgrims when they reached the holy place. But it is interesting to see some traces of graffiti – crosses carved on the stone walls. Also the floor of the cathedral slopes downhill (that is, it is not completely level). This made it easier to wash the floor if people were ill or suffering from bad stomachs after their long journeys!

Pilgrimages remained popular throughout the Middle Ages, but when, during the 1530s Henry VIII decided to break away from the Church of Rome, he ordered the destruction of all sacred places – the monasteries, the abbeys and the wells. For a time pilgrimages came to an end. But today, once again, some people go on pilgrimages to places such as Bardsey Island and Penrhys, and especially, of course, to St Davids.

pilgrim springtime

Sunlight on window panes
Tells us the time,
The old bells of Clynnog
Wake all with their chime,
The stream sings a song as it wends on its way
In praise of Saint David's Day.

Along pilgrim ways
Trod by Beuno of old,
Though winter still clings
And the wind is so cold,
The memories of miracles are in the sun's ray,
The miracles of Saint David's Day.

Scented with flowers
The chapel lies hid.
Tired pilgrims still seek it
As they always did,
And brightly on T-shirts the daffodils sway
To the tunes of Saint David's Day.

Adapted from 'Gwanwyn y Pererinion', by the children of Ysgol Rhostryfan and Iwan Llwyd

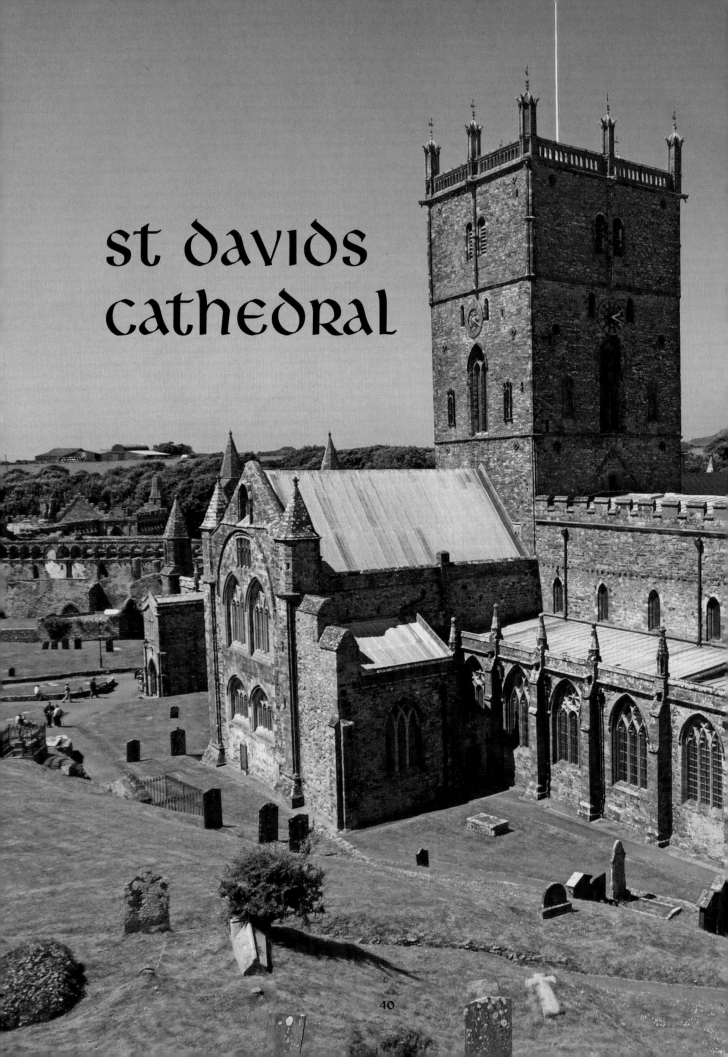

st davids cathedral

St Davids Cathedral is one of the best-known buildings in Wales. As well as being the seat of the Bishop of St Davids ('cathedral' comes from the Greek word *cathedra* which means 'seat'), it is also the parish church of the city of St Davids.

Of course, this is not the original church that was built by David and his followers. The first church was destroyed by fire in the year 645. The Vikings attacked the area in the tenth and eleventh centuries, and they supposedly destroyed the church buildings that were built after the fire. By the twelfth century – in the time of Bernard, the first Norman bishop – yet another church had been built. Only a few stones of that church now remain.

In 1181 or 1182 work began on rebuilding the cathedral. It took hundreds of years to complete. The purple sandstone that was used in its construction came from the rocks of Caerbwdi nearby. This stone is still used to this day to repair the cathedral walls.

the story of the cathedral

In 1275 a new shrine was built, because the original shrine was stolen from the cathedral in 1089. Pilgrims would come to see St David's bones, which had only recently been 'rediscovered'. Today, in the cathedral, in the wall between Holy Trinity Chapel and the Altar, you can still see the little oak chest that holds the bones of two saints – a tall saint (David) and a short saint (Justinian).

Towards the end of the thirteenth century, an octagonal bell tower was built to house the cathedral bells. Because the cathedral lies in a valley, the bell tower had to be a little higher so that the sound of the bells carried further. The Tower Gate was added to it in the following century. The oak ceiling dates from the thirteenth century and the oak may well have been brought over the sea from Ireland.

The Bishop's Palace is now a ruin, but in the middle of the fourteenth century, when most if it was constructed by Bishop Henry Gower, it was a magnificent building. The bishops used to live in the east wing, and important pilgrims – including the king of England – would lodge in the south wing.

The cathedral was badly damaged in 1648, when the Parliamentary soldiers came to St Davids to remove tons of lead from its roof. So, for a long time, parts of the cathedral were roofless. The soldiers also destroyed the stained glass windows, the organ and the bells, amongst other things. But gradually, over the next three hundred years, the damage was repaired – for example by the architect John Nash in 1793 and by Sir George Gilbert Scott in 1862. During the twentieth century, more repair work had to be done. Woodwork that was riddled with woodworm had to be replaced, and new bells were hung in the Tower Gate.

By today, St Davids Cathedral attracts large numbers of visitors throughout the year and many concerts are held there. As well as admiring the cathedral itself, people come to see the graves of famous Welshmen: Rhys ap Gruffydd, one of the most important princes of south Wales; Edmund Tudor, father of Henry VII; and Gerald of Wales. But, of course, the main purpose of the cathedral is to hold services. People from the parish of St Davids attend the services, as do people from the diocese of St Davids (Pembrokeshire, Ceredigion and Carmarthenshire), and people throughout Wales.

celebrating st david's day in ysgol gymraeg dewi sant, llanelli

This school, along with many others throughout Wales, believes that St David's Day is a chance to remind ourselves to be good Welsh men and women throughout the year. Here are the children's opinions of what we should do to be good Welsh men and women:

- Speak Welsh to our family and friends wherever possible
- Support all Welsh sports teams
- Help to keep the language alive by teaching Welsh to others
- Be proud of the Welsh flag and the leek
- Be aware of the fascinating history of our country
- Look after our beautiful environment and appreciate the fine scenery
- Wear the Welsh costume with pride
- Compete in eisteddfodau
- Welcome visitors from other countries and respect them
- Never forget our Welshness wherever we are in the world

leeks

Traditionally we wear leeks and eat leek soup on St David's Day. Why?

Some say, for example, that David himself used to eat leeks. This is quite possible, for we know that David and his monks used to cultivate the land at Glyn Rhosyn. Because leeks are fairly easy to grow, leek soup would probably have been on David's menu.

The first time that leeks were worn was perhaps in the year 633, about fifty years after David's death. The story goes that Cadwallon ap Cadfan, King of Gwynedd, was preparing his soldiers for battle against the Saxons. But there was one problem: the Saxons and the Welsh wore almost identical clothes. There was a danger the Welsh might kill each other instead of the Saxons! So, to make sure that the Welsh could recognise each other and distinguish between themselves and the Saxons, Cadwallon gave each of his men a leek to wear in his hat.

wearing leeks

It is also said that Welsh people grew leeks for luck, happiness and to drive away evil spirits. People believed that leeks would help them live forever. So soldiers used to rub leeks on their bodies to protect themselves in battle and keep them safe. Maybe the enemy kept away because of the smell of the leeks, and that is how the soldiers' lives were saved!

Over the centuries, the colours of the leek – green and white – became the royal colours of Wales. There are many references to Welshmen wearing leeks in battle, such as at the battle of Crécy in 1346. In his play *Henry V*, William Shakespeare refers to Welsh bowmen wearing leeks in the Battle of Agincourt in 1415.

When Henry Tudor, the first of the Tudor kings, became King of England in 1485, the colours green and white featured on his coat of arms. Henry Tudor's family came from Anglesey and Pembrokeshire, so he probably used the colours of the leek to show his connection with Wales.

The Physicians of Myddfai, famous doctors from Carmarthenshire, used leeks to cure people. They used to make medicines and ointments from plants and minerals, and used leeks to put on bruises and to heal broken bones.

These days we eat leek soup and wear leeks to show that we're Welsh. This doesn't only happen on St David's Day. Nowadays we play rugby against other countries instead of fighting them in battle like the Welshmen of long ago, but it is still important for us to identify ourselves. So Welsh supporters wear leeks of various sizes – some of them huge!

It is worth remembering these lines by the poet Eifion Wyn, which remind us that we should be good Welsh people all the year round, not only on St David's Day:

Wear a leek in your cap

And wear it in your heart.

(*Gwisg genhinen yn dy gap.*

A gwisg hi yn dy galon.)

GROWING LEEKS

One gardener famous for growing leeks is Medwyn Williams from Anglesey. He has won many gold medals for his vegetables at the Chelsea Show.

Growing large leeks is quite a long process. In September Medwyn takes leeks that have already been growing for a year, and plants them in pots. By the following May the leeks are flowering and are trying to run to seed. Every flower must be cut off. When this happens, the leek goes into a state of shock and throws out small leeks from its head, so it looks like a green brush. Medwyn pulls these off and plants them at the end of autumn in a heated greenhouse. They stay in the greenhouse throughout the winter and then Medwyn moves them to larger pots. Around the middle of April, Medwyn plants them out.

What sort of soil is good for leeks? Well, good quality soil with plenty of drainage. It must also be prepared, and enriched with farm dung that has been left to rot down for two to three years.

How big are Medwyn's leeks after all this work? Well, they're huge – more than two metres in length with a diameter of over 10 cm. They weigh several kilograms – enough to make a supply of soup that will last for weeks!

leek soup

Soup or *cawl* is a traditional food that used to be eaten all winter. Nowadays it is especially associated with St David's Day. This recipe makes enough for 6 servings. To make vegetarian soup, leave out the lamb.

Ingredients

About 1kg neck of lamb
250g onions
250g carrots
250g parsnips
250g swedes or turnips
1kg potatoes
3 leeks
salt and pepper

Method

1 First remove as much fat as possible from the meat, then boil gently in a saucepan of water for an hour.

2 Remove the fat from the surface of the liquid (it is easier to do this when the liquid has cooled).

3 Peel and chop the vegetables and add them to the lamb.

4 Add a little salt and pepper.

5 Put the lid on the saucepan and boil till the vegetables are cooked through.

making a leek

You will need: Two sheets of thin A4 card, one green and the other white ▪ A pencil ▪ A pair of small scissors ▪ Sellotape ▪ A safety pin

Place the two sheets of paper with the long sides facing you. Place about 5 cm of the white sheet over the green one and tape both together with a long piece of sellotape.

Roll the card around a pencil to form a tube.

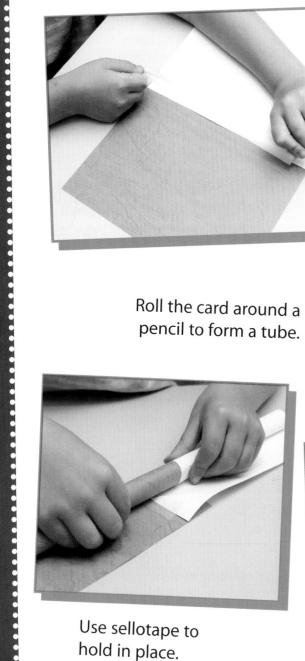

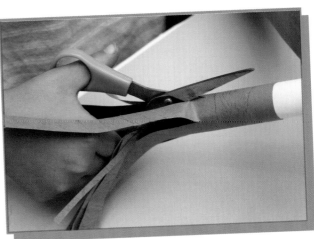

Use sellotape to hold in place.

Cut straight lines in the green part about 8 cm in length and 2 cm apart to make 'leaves'.

To make the leaves curl, pull the blade of the scissors along the strips. (You could practice this on strips of card beforehand.)

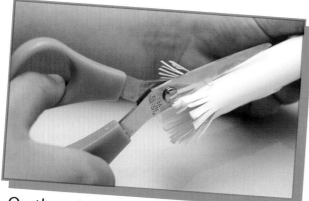

On the white part, cut straight lines of about 0.5 cm to form roots.

Use sellotape to stick a safety pin on top of the other piece of sellotape.

leek people!

How about making little costumes for your leeks? Here are some examples of leek people.

the daffodil

It was probably the Romans who brought daffodils to Britain. They used them to heal wounds. This proved particularly useful when many soldiers were wounded in battle.

Today, more than fifteen hundred years after the Romans left Wales, the flower is still being used to cure people. Daffodils produce galanthamine, which can be made into a drug to treat people who are suffering from Alzheimer's. Very little of this drug is available, so it is very expensive. Research has shown that the daffodils of mid-Wales (where the winters are coldest) produce most galanthamine. It is to be hoped that this will lead to a new business venture, and help sick people at the same time.

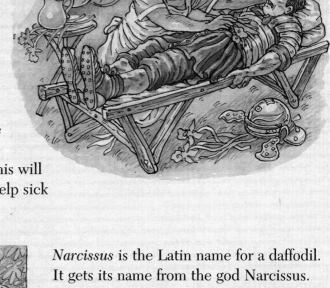

Narcissus is the Latin name for a daffodil. It gets its name from the god Narcissus. While looking into a pool of water, Narcissus fell in love with his own reflection, tumbled into the water and drowned! According to the legend, a daffodil grew on that very spot.

The logo of
Glamorgan
Cricket Club

Many types of wild daffodil grow in Wales:

✿ *Narcissus pseudonarcissus*. These grow mainly in Gwent. You'll see them flowering in Margaret's Wood Nature Reserve, near Monmouth, at the end of March and the beginning of April.

✿ *Narcissus obvallaris* or 'Tenby daffodil'. These grow throughout Pembrokeshire.

✿ *Derwydd* – a form of double daffodil.

Over 26,000 types of daffodil have been bred as garden flowers. Every spring, the National Trust holds a Daffodil Day at Llanerchaeron, near Aberaeron, where several of the varieties are displayed. Many of them grow in the grounds of the mansion.

Narcissus pseudonarcissus

Narcissus obvallaris

Derwydd

wearing the daffodil

The daffodil is one of the few flowers that bloom around St David's Day. Perhaps that is why daffodils are also called 'David's Flowers' or 'David's Leeks'.

Although leeks have been worn for a very long time, it was only in the Victorian Age that people began to wear daffodils on St David's Day. At that time many Welsh people had moved to live in the big English cities, such as Manchester and London. It was while celebrating St David's Day in their Welsh societies that they began to wear the daffodil – because it was prettier and sweeter-smelling than the poor old leek! Nowadays the daffodil is possibly more popular than the leek.

The Great Western Railway company used to arrange special trips to the countryside in springtime, so that townspeople could see the daffodils. These came to an end in the middle of the twentieth century.

People used to lay daffodils on family graves around St David's Day, but today we have large bunches in our houses instead. Many local councils plant them on roadsides, roundabouts, and around the signposts that welcome visitors to towns and villages.

Here are four lines adapted from a poem by I.D. Hooson, which describes the flower, its green leaves and its golden head:

> 'No happier flower was ever seen
> With cloak of green and golden hair
> A-dancing in the wind and rain
> To a hidden piper's sweetest air.'
> *(Ni welwyd un erioed mor llon,*
> *A'th fantell werdd a'th euraidd rudd,*
> *Yn dawnsio yn y gwynt a'r glaw,*
> *I bibau pêr rhyw gerddor cudd.)*

the flower of spring

The bells of David tell us
That the time has come at last,
A time to dance
For the wind is warm
And winter now has passed.

Our saint's star shimmers brightly
Through dark and gloomy trees,
Through branches gaunt,
Through withered fern,
Through the rustle of dried-up
leaves.

The proclamation candles hail
The new strength in the earth;
The springs once again
That can wash away pain;
The children of the present day
Who know our history's worth.

*Adapted from 'Blodyn
y Gwanwyn' by the children
of Ysgol Llanbedrog and
Myrddin ap Dafydd*

the daffodils of st davids

Long ago, people would earn a penny or two in springtime by gathering wild daffodils and selling them in the local market. The business of selling daffodils is still going strong today. The largest daffodil farm in Wales happens to be within a stone's throw of St Davids Cathedral. Every year the Perkins family farm sells around 1 million flowers and forty thousand bulbs. These are not wild daffodils, but commercial varieties with names such as 'Touchmaster' and 'Golden Harvest'.

From the end of January onwards the flowers must be gathered before they have opened. There are no machines for harvesting daffodils, so each flower must be picked by hand, which is very hard work! If you go to a market in south Wales in February, the daffodils on sale are probably from St Davids. Each year about a third of all the flowers – whole fields – are not picked, because they are growing from young bulbs.

At the beginning of July, after the leaves have wilted, the bulbs must be lifted. They are brought to a shed, where they are cleaned and graded according to size. Then they must be left to dry in boxes for a while, before the biggest are put in bags ready to be sold. The smallest bulbs are replanted in the fields, once the soil has cooled, around the middle of September.

The daffodil bulb keeps on growing, and even in July, next year's flower can be seen in it, already formed.

It is very appropriate that daffodils should be grown so close to St Davids. Also, the cathedral itself looks at its best in springtime with all the daffodils that grow around it.

making a daffodil

You will need:

2 pieces of card, A4 size, one green piece and one yellow. A smaller piece of card for the star-shaped template.
Pencil
Felt pen
Long ruler
Small pair of scissors
Sellotape
Glue
Safety pin

Measure a 3 cm wide strip along the long side of the yellow card and cut it out.

With a felt pen, draw a star shape on the smaller piece of card and cut it out to make your template.

Place the template on the yellow card and trace a shape around it with the pencil. Cut out the shape.

Roll the narrow strip of yellow card to form a tube and close it with a piece of tape. Make four 1 cm deep cuts in the tube to form tabs.

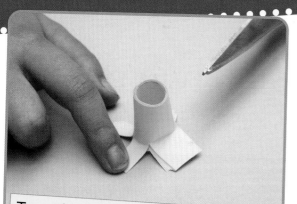

Turn the tube over and make a frill for the centre of the flower by making small cuts about half a centimetre deep.

Glue the tabs onto the star shape.

Roll the green card around the pencil to form a tube, and close it with a piece of tape. Squash one end and cut it to make a leaf tip shape.

Make long cuts down the stem to within 5 cm of the bottom to create a leaf effect.

Stick the flower to the stem. Use sellotape to stick a safety pin to the back of the daffodil's stem. You could also make several flowers to fill a vase or to make a lovely display.

dressing up on st david's day

Today in our school it's St David's Day.
A hairy monster is coming our way.
It's Gelert the dog, and hard on his heels
Comes a Cydweli lady with liquorice wheels.
A farmer in clogs clump-clumps down the road
Followed by Owain Glyndŵr with his sword,
Hywel walks in with a silvery axe,
While Wali Tomos shouts, "Come on, you backs!"
Here's Gavin Henson, hair spiky with gel;
Saint Dwynwen with hearts and a halo as well;
William Morgan who's tugging his beard,
As he translates the Bible, word after word;
Siân Lloyd with her tidy and well-pressed locks;
Jac y Jwc with his trousers not reaching his socks.
Llywelyn the Great who's mighty and proud
And great Bryn Terfel who sings out loud;
With pride in their hearts they all shout "Hooray!"
And wave the Red Dragon on David's Day.

Adapted from 'Gwisg Gŵyl Ddewi' by Years 4 and 5,
Ysgol y Gorlan, Tremadog
and Myrddin ap Dafydd

the welsh costume

Nowadays, on St David's Day, many children go to school in Welsh costume. But what is the Welsh costume? To find the answer we must go back two or three hundred years. At that time you could tell where people came from just by looking at their clothes. We can't do that today, because lots of people throughout the world wear the same sort of clothes.

Before the days of the Industrial Revolution, there weren't any large clothes factories. Many people made their own clothes at home, or were given them as part of their wages. People kept sheep for wool, and the poor gathered wool from the hedges. After carding, dyeing, spinning and weaving the wool, the cloth was ready to be cut up into garments. Every country, and more or less every region, had its own patterns, so clothes varied from place to place. Eighteenth-century and early-nineteenth-century clothes are the traditional dress of most European countries. These are the ones that people wear today when they celebrate national holidays, such as St David's Day, or compete in Llangollen Eisteddfod, for instance.

welsh women's costume

So what is traditional Welsh costume? Women used to wear clothes similar to the ones that little girls wear on St David's Day. These included:

■ a tall hat – which was fashionable in towns in the seventeenth century. But straw or felt hats were popular in some areas.

■ a white bonnet – worn under the hat and edged with lace.

■ a skirt – of striped woollen cloth.

■ a petticoat – sometimes this was like a feather quilt, and very warm.

■ an apron – also made of woollen cloth, and similar to a modern apron, but larger.

■ a blouse – usually white.

■ a bedgown – a short jacket with a long tail.

■ a shawl – some shawls were small, others large enough to swaddle a baby. These were called 'nursing shawls'. The mother could nurse the baby while she did the housework. Woollen shawls with a checked pattern were made at home, but shawls with more intricate patterns such as paisley were bought.

■ a cloak – it was large and covered everything. In north Wales and Ceredigion the cloak was usually black or dark blue, but in south and mid Wales it was usually red.

■ stockings – knitted from white, grey or black wool. In north Wales they were mainly knitted from the wool of black sheep.

■ shoes – wooden shoes, or clogs, because leather shoes were expensive. Nowadays people wear clogs to dance the clog dance, but years ago they were everyday wear. Those who did own a pair of leather shoes would often wear clogs to make a journey on foot, then take them off and put on the leather shoes just before reaching their destination, to avoid dirtying the leather.

You could tell where people came from by looking at the patterns and colours of the cloth. For example the colour red, made from a dye derived from cockles, was popular in coastal areas. People thought that red woollen cloth was warmer and good for colds. The French tried to land in Pembrokeshire in 1797, but were frightened off when they saw people dressed in red on the coast. The Frenchmen thought they were soldiers, whereas in actual fact they were women dressed in red cloaks. In mid and north Wales lichen gathered from the rocks and trees was used to dye the wool, so the cloth was darker.

Jemima Nicholas

In the nineteenth century, when Welsh women were starting to turn their backs on traditional dress, Lady Llanover, in Gwent, urged them to keep wearing it. As we have already seen, there were many different costumes in Wales at the time, but when tourists began visiting Wales, artists began to concentrate on one type of Welsh costume. This is the one we see on postcards and souvenirs of Wales, and this is the one that is now sold in shops and markets around St David's Day.

men's costume

But what about the men? They wore corduroy
trousers, a woollen shirt and a brown jerkin. On
their feet they had wooden clogs and the woollen
socks that their wives knitted. Coal-miners' dress
was rather different. They wore dark blue with
leather jerkins. They also had leather caps with
peaks for holding candles, which was their only
light underground.

It is said that a hermit called John James from
Llangeler in Carmarthenshire used to wear a
woollen kilt at the beginning of the twentieth
century. He claimed it was the traditional dress
of the Britons. Nowadays Welsh tartan kilts are
very popular and *Welsh Tartan Centres* was set up in 1996.
'St David's Tartan' was created after studying patterns of old shawls on postcards. It was
a great success, with many men buying kilts to wear at weddings or on special
occasions. The Cambrian Woollen Mill near Llanwrtyd was kept very busy.

Then came a demand for fifty new tartans. Each one is named after a Welsh surname – e.g. Jones, Davies, Evans, Owen, Roberts and so on. Shops in south Wales sell kilts, as do other places throughout the world, from Disney in Florida to Sydney in Australia.

These days, adults and children wear all sorts of clothes on St David's Day to show that they're Welsh. They wear rugby shirts or red dragon dresses, or even dress up as King Arthur's knights and Owain Glyndŵr. Even so, the Welsh 'traditional' costume still holds its own.

welsh cakes

**Welsh cakes are traditional St David's Day fare.
This mixture will make about 45 cakes.**

Ingredients

500g self-raising flour
125g butter or margarine
125g vegetable fat
200g sugar
200g currants
2 eggs

Method

1 Place the griddle on the hob to heat.

2 Sieve the self-raising flour into a large bowl.

3 Rub the butter or margarine and the vegetable fat into the flour till it looks like breadcrumbs.

4 Add the sugar and the currants.

5 Make a well in the centre of the mixture. Beat two eggs, and pour them into the well.

6 With a fork, mix gradually, till the mixture forms a large ball, which can be lifted cleanly from the bowl. If you don't want to roll it out and make the cakes immediately, the ball of dough can be kept in the fridge for a day or two.

7 Sprinkle a little flour on the rolling surface.

8 Cut the dough more or less in half, and then roll with a rolling pin until it forms a large circle about half to three quarters of a centimetre thick.

9 Use small round cutters to cut out the cakes.

10 Place the Welsh cakes carefully on the griddle, and cook for about 3 minutes each side till they turn light brown. But keep an eye on them, in case they burn!

11 Leave to cool, and serve with a sprinkling of sugar. Some people spread butter on them too.

the red dragon flag

The Romans brought the red dragon to Wales. They used a dragon as their emblem. (*Draco* is the Latin for 'dragon'.) The dragon's head was made of metal and set on top of a pole. Strips of cloth, to represent fire, would issue from its mouth, along with smoke and the noise of whistling. When the Romans left Wales in the fifth century, some of their officers and their dragon emblems may have stayed on.

The Saxons had a white dragon on their banner, and one of Wales's best-known folk tales tells of a fight between the red dragon of Wales and the white dragon of England. King Vortigern (Gwrtheyrn) was trying to build a new castle in Gwynedd, but each time he built walls on top of the foundations, the whole structure would fall down before daybreak. Vortigern had no idea what was happening, so he asked his wise men for their advice. They told him to search for a boy without a father. The boy would have to be sacrificed and his blood poured over the foundations. Only then could the building work go ahead. After searching far and wide, a boy of this kind was found in Carmarthenshire; he was playing with a ball. His name was Emrys Wledig. Emrys proved at once that he was an exceptional boy, by telling the wise men that there was a lake beneath the foundations of the castle. Two dragons lived in this lake, one red and one white. Each night they moved and brought the walls tumbling down.

Vortigern and his men dug deep into the earth and, indeed, they found the lake just as Emrys had said. As the water level dropped, the red dragon and the white dragon appeared. They both woke up, and began to fight fiercely. The red dragon won in the end.

Vortigern went on to build a castle in another spot, called Nant Gwrtheyrn, but Emrys decided to build his castle on the hill where the dragons had fought. That hill is still called Dinas Emrys.

Perhaps the fight between the red dragon and the white symbolises the fighting that took place through the centuries between the Welsh and the English. They say that King Arthur carried the red dragon flag when he went to battle against the Saxons.

'the red dragon leads the way'

To praise their leaders' strength and bravery, Welsh poets often compared them to dragons. After all, what can be fiercer than a dragon? For example, Meilyr Brydydd said that Gruffydd ap Cynan was 'like the dragon of Gwynedd'. And this is how Llywelyn ap Gruffudd was described by Gruffudd ab yr Ynad Coch: 'Head of a leader, a dragon's head had he.' (*Pen dragon, pen draig oedd arnaw.*)

When Henry Tudor from Wales defeated King Richard III on Bosworth field in 1485, he apparently had a picture of a red dragon on a huge flag. The dragon was also on the royal coat of arms of the Tudors, but it disappeared in the time of King James I and was replaced by a unicorn.

The Red Dragon reappeared as the royal emblem of Wales in 1807. Welsh societies would often use it as a logo. It only became an official symbol about fifty years ago. The motto 'The Red Dragon leads the way' (*Y ddraig goch ddyry cychwyn*) comes from a poem by Deio ab Ieuan Ddu, in which the poet asks Siôn ap Rhys, Glynneath, for a gift of a bull.

the golden dragon of Owain Glyndŵr

There is another flag, which is associated with Owain Glyndŵr – the Golden Lion rampant. Apparently, when Owain's men attacked Caernarfon Castle in 1401, 1403 and 1404, they marched behind a banner bearing a golden lion on a white background. Owain Glyndŵr met with failure each time. But an extraordinary thing happened in 2004, six hundred years after Glyndŵr last attempt. Permission was granted for Glyndŵr's banner to be flown from one of the castle towers every year from henceforth. Members of Llysgenhadaeth Glyndŵr (Glyndŵr's Embassy) marched through the streets of Caernarfon. They went into the castle to raise the flag and, in their colourful costumes, they 'presented the Golden Dragon to the people of Wales'. No doubt Owain Glyndŵr would have been delighted!

the dragon today

The dragon is still used in many logos today. For example:
- the head and wings of the dragon, as part of the logo of Llanelli Scarlets rugby team
- two red dragons on the badge of Wrexham football team
- the company 'Pendragon Furniture'
- the Welsh Tourist Board's information centres

the flag of st david

The Flag of St David is based on the arms of the bishops of St Davids: a gold cross on a black background. On the flag there are five cinquefoils, a flower with five petals which represents the rose that used to grow along the coast of Pembrokeshire, known as 'David's Rose'. Gold and black were the colours of Rhys ap Tewdwr, king of south Wales, when Rhygyfarch wrote *Buchedd Dewi* in the eleventh century. This flag has been in use since 1939.

celebrating
st david's day today

Nowadays there are lots of different events and activities to mark St David's Day. For example:

- a St David's Day concert
- *cawl* (soup) and songs
- an eisteddfod
- a lecture on Welsh history or on St David
- a dinner with a guest speaker
- the St David's Day 5km race in Bute Park, Cardiff
- the Guto Fun Race, Aberystwyth

The Bishop of St Davids holding a St David's Day Service

Every 1st of March Ysgol Dewi Sant (St David's School) Llanelli, celebrates both St David's Day and the school's birthday. The school opened on the 1st of March 1947. A special service starts off the day, with each class contributing an item. Artwork is displayed in the morning and prizes are given to the winners. The highlight is the chairing ceremony, when the adjudicator names the winning author. At the sound of the 'national horn' (*corn gwlad*), the winner gets to his or her feet and is awarded the chair for the best poem or prose work of the year.

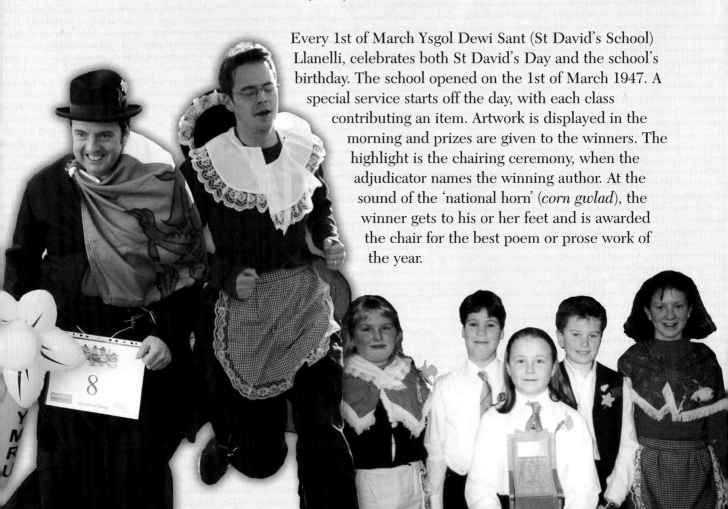

S4C celebrates St David's Day by holding the Song for Wales competition every year, and the choral competition – Côr Cymru – every two years.

Many Welsh-language books are published around St David's Day, which is celebrated around the same time as World Book Day.

In 2005 the Welsh singer Aled Jones launched his autobiography on St David's Day. Special foods and produce are launched, for example Dewi Sant Ale and Dewi Sant ice cream.

St David's Day celebrations at St Davids

st david's day parades

For several years there has been a parade in Cardiff on St David's Day. This is an opportunity for all the people of Wales to come together to celebrate, as the Irish do. There is also a parade in Colwyn Bay. In 2005 it was part of a week of events to mark St David's Day, which included a fashion show, a singing festival, a service, a concert and light entertainment (*noson lawen*).

The Colwyn Bay parade

the name dewi

Dewi is Welsh for David. It is still a popular name today, almost fifteen hundred years after the time of Dewi Sant.

Two pupils of Ysgol Gymraeg Dewi Sant called Dewi

Dewi Pws

St David's Day
in Gilfach Ddu

They're still here, the daffodils,
amid the rubble of the quarry,
golden glow on grey slate,
in vases in the Fountain café,
reflected in each plate.

They're still here, the daffodils,
still witness to the chipping,
the *trafal* and the steel bit,
the singing in the shed's warmth,
men's laughter and sweat.

They're still here, the daffodils,
still nodding to jackdaw boys,
to Llŷn and Anglesey men,
who once turned this hard *bargen*
into a warm friendly den.

And today we see dragons on the slates
and cawl, harpist and choir;
step through yesterday's doorway
and draw close to the fire;
in our hearts are the daffodils.

Adapted from 'Dathlu Gŵyl Ddewi yn y Gilfach
Ddu' by the children of Ysgol Dolbadarn with
Meirion McIntyre Huws and Myrddin ap Dafydd.

celebrating st david's day overseas

St David's Day is an opportunity for people living overseas to think of Wales. Many Welsh Societies throughout the world meet to celebrate in their own way:

Taiwan

- The Welsh American Society of Northern California holds a Cymanfa Ganu (Singing Festival), which is attended by about two hundred people. At the end of the festival, they have a Welsh tea.

- Many societies, in America and throughout the world, hold St David's Day dinners. These include the Welsh Society of Pittsburgh, Pennsylvania, the Welsh Society of Arizona and the Welsh Society of Hong Kong.

- The Welsh people of Melbourne, Australia, hold a Prynhawn Llawen – an afternoon of entertainment – consisting of a dinner, a talk, songs, harp music, folk groups, and poetry and prose-readings in Welsh.

Greece

- Manchester Welsh Society holds a concert featuring a male voice choir from Wales, and other items. At the end of the concert, everyone sings a popular Welsh hymn and then – of course! – *Hen Wlad fy Nhadau* (Land of my Fathers). Welsh chapels in the area celebrate by listening to a St David's Day sermon delivered by a minister from Wales, or by holding a dinner or a celebration in the chapel itself with entertainment provided by the members.

- The Welsh Society of Taiwan held a concert in 2004 with Bryn Terfel as guest artist.

- In 2005, the Chicago Welsh Society (the Chicago Tafia Welsh Society) celebrated first of all by watching the Welsh rugby team beat France. Then they had a St David's Day dinner and a special auction of Welsh goods, including items from Aur Rhiannon (Rhiannon Welsh Gold), St David's Tartan, music, and a picture of the Welsh rugby team beating England. They also visited children in a Chicago hospital and gave each of them a little dragon, to encourage them to fight like dragons against their illness.

- Foods from Wales are promoted overseas during Welsh Weeks, for example in New York, Dubai, Paris and Brussels.

- Disneyland Paris celebrates St David's Day, because one of the managers is Welsh.

Canada

Hong Kong

Jordan

index